CANTICLE
FOR REMNANT DAYS

Canticle for Remnant Days

Poems
Jane C. Miller

Pond Road Press
North Truro, Massachusetts

Cover art: *Conflict No. 1,* by Judy Kirpich
Copyright © 2023 Judy Kirpich all rights reserved.
www.judykirpich.com

Cover art photograph: Mark Gulesian

Book design and composition by Mary Ann Larkin
and Patric Pepper.

ISBN: 978-1-7336574-3-3

Library of Congress Control Number: 2023948463

Further acknowledgments follow page 90.

1 2 3 4 5 6 7 8 9 10

Pond Road Press
P.O. Box 30
North Truro, Massachusetts 02652

patric.pepper@yahoo.com

Available through major online booksellers, Ingram Content
Group distribution and through Pond Road Press directly.

For my family

Contents

One

Heading West on I-80

So many deer die in poems, I am due
      to hit one. I stop

      on the lookout as the sun sets
on my face, air hot

with road tar. No job and help wanted
      for what escapes me.

      In the bowl of a hill rimmed with firs,
a doe stalls to chew grass.

Her white tail dismisses
      the gossip of flies. Doesn't she know

      someone is always out for blood, men
will field dress a deer fresh-hit.

Sixteen-wheelers downshift. Far removed
      from their thumping decels, she

      does not look up. She stays in place
as she pulls up roots, shadows lengthening

to reach her. Once, our hands so hungry
      we filled them with each other in the dark—

darkness, tunnels ahead, ash where light hits.

After an Argument with a Friend

The sun still crossing the Atlantic, plows
night before it. Fishing boats

off the Azores muscle for blue
marlin. I wake in darkness

Rothko painted; eyes open-shut,
everything blue-black, nothing

certain. Even the thinnest yarn
in a microscope yields a ragged edge—

I am wrong about the hour.

Of the Safe House, Now Empty

Boxed by a calendar, those blank days a numbing countdown

where everything untouched had texture: the sky's darkness

sponge-scrubbed by snow, anemic reflection

of the eclipsed moon; on the roof, a blackboard astrology

scratched by birds, weathered walls spun straight as

hay's weak promise; by the entrance, a dark spillway

broken by a white skyline, and prone in snow's pumice,

a single tree limb, greening leaves sharp as palette knives.

Where the door framed us, we were a postcard

valentine no one saw the back of. If there is a story

here, it is how the world we left still touched us.

Burrs

I didn't know love came
with asterisks. That's the lesson.

Violets wild on the lawn, scars
a million stars make in the dark—

our mistakes accumulate.
Why have I let them

guide me? Tell me why
I always confuse know

with no, my tongue that
staples the soft lamb's ear.

Advice to My Six-Year-Old Self

Get out from under the kitchen table.
Plenty of time for that later when no one
bothers to pull you out of the hole where
a word problem holds you captive.

Years from now, if a train leaves Omaha, let it
never come back to the paper where
your pencil stops before Wichita. How to solve for x
when y makes no sense is a koan that rubs
its antlers clean as moonlight on the garage.

You're in first grade, your days already
numbered by failure to understand
equivalence, where letters can be math

or love. You scrawl *I hade you*
when Mother refuses to help.
She pushes Swiss steak around and laughs—
you will always be alone

with your problems. How many times have I
been under a table with sums I can't total, empties
from the night before souring the counter.

Wall marks that notched how much I grew
stopped at Algebra II. Just wait, girl—

you will learn to care less. So much more
you won't understand, your mother

who knew to push back—
the paper, its dark smudges,
friction erasing rage into a hole.

Squeeze Play

I leave my husband at the Derby to watch the Phillies
lose. At the bar, men trade black lung for cancer;
their glasses fill from a hole in the bottom,
a magnet drops & seals. Everyone has

a right to their own destruction, to never
say when. Game won, he washes away
the smoke that clings, easy for him. I have
two breakfasts, biscuits smothered in sausage

gravy, fattening arteries tight with age. Always
careless, I take for granted my flawed decisions, regret
that wears self-pity like a merit badge: the heart
just once wants to be held by someone else—

in a surgeon's hands, the limitless air cool, no lungs
to fill, no ribs to clang its weathered bell against.
When my father's heart sat in a stainless pan, did it

register all the beeps & waving monitors, the calls
for instruments & suction. Did it savor its vacation,
the sonorous voice stilled: broken-open vault
stretched out on a cold table.

I've felt mine curse what hurts, flip with laughter,
slow me into sleep's calm & thought
nothing of it. Isn't all its hard work a form of love

I was taught as a child. My father's hand
would squeeze mine four times: "Do you love me?"
& I'd squeeze back "Yes I do." He'd press "Do you?"
My final *yes* all the hurt I could put into it.

Changing Room at Alexander's, 1964

We didn't expect company.
Along walls of mirrors, women struggled

in and out of clothes: girdles snapped
to hose, boobs overflowing

cone brassieres. My mother put on
a casual air. At eight, old enough

to know I'd make it worse if someone
caught me looking, I tried to look

where someone wasn't, but they were
everywhere in triplicate, surveying

their fronts and rears in mirrors,
pretending to be alone.

What they came in, cast off like
fur Selkie seals unzipped—

how I wish we had chanced upon them
here, dancing naked and carefree as myth.

When did they learn shame, these budget
shoppers looking for glamour

in Paramus: in their eyes the eyes
of men, the light harsh, unforgiving.

Family Quartet

Everybody plays—
mom's voice high and thin
as the rim of a wine glass,

my sister and I, woodwinds
we practice at home. After dinner
Dad performs drills, beating time

with his leather strop, a tune-up
when it isn't my turn, for my little sister
at the kitchen chair holding on

for the downstroke, our mother
off somewhere and me upstairs
in bed, the winter moon

through thin glass a spotlight
on me, on what I have watched

play out: my sister's braced arms,
her small hands clutching the chair back,
she looks past slats at dirty cracks

in the red brick linoleum, at crumbs
from dinner rolls, her back facing him
I can't stop, his leather belt in hand,

my little sister plays her high notes
through its notches, again. I try
to warm her side of the bed.

The Body's Certainty

I felt the hand of my mother
patting my right shoulder just outside the covers

the night after she died, and yes it could have been
the heater blowing its warmth my way, or perhaps

fatigue releasing muscles from their ropes, even
an angel's touch and go, if you believe—

but I know with the body's certainty born
of her body, that she came to console, not

to explain or forgive (as her endearments
sometimes turned, or turned to relief,

her silhouette down the hall stealing away)
—once love becomes a habit, sure as

a dream bleeds from darkness into day,
hard to break, even when broken

Afterward

The dock is almost under again.
Since you died, days press their throttling tide
and each night darkness pours its panic
marbles underfoot. I walk the house,

let myself out to prowl the sleeping cove,
come back and stand at the refrigerator,
searching in the alien light of its kitchen moon
for solace, but there is only water.

Night Swim

The pool's underwater light shines
like a moon. I frog the water, think of nothing
but what I want. Back home
my dog hangs his head over the sofa edge

like a gargoyle. A cool wind shivers my skin.
Dad, you can't know how it felt to slide you,
heavy as bone-chipped sand, from a plastic bag
into dug earth. Your empty condo echoes.

Water licks at me insistent as a dog
wanting to be pet, and I submerge. Who's to say
death is the end of habits that make us
happy or misunderstood? In this smoky light, others

return. Doc, who always swam laps at night,
methodically crawls above me. The legs
of the morning ladies stalk the shallow end,
their too-big trophy rings sparkle like exit lights
on the floor. Out of breath, I hang on the pool's rough edge.

In the dark community room, your best friends
Pete and Stew, Hawaiian shirts in tatters, Jack Daniels
in hand; Marty brushes dirt from her collarbone
where she wore statement pins; Vince's ponytail so long

now it's a scarf. You are center stage, holding
your titanium knee and tibia like an MC. Alive,
you had no time for my what-ifs, my moodiness.

Life of the party, I want you back.
I want you back at the window of 101-C calling down

to the pool ladies, their faces upturned
like sunflowers. I want your barrel-chested whinny,

your absent-minded singing, half-whistling *I Love
Paris in the Springtime* on repeat, your strong hand
stroking the gap between my pointer and thumb.

A timer turns off the pool light. The flagpole rope
clangs a curfew. Palms shir like forked tongues.

Rule of Jaw

Everyone hated Chloe, the terrier we bought
to teach you how to love—forget
her messes, the crate door she banged
open and shut, her manic
pull at the leash, her wants and
flaws we took as our own as we did
with you who didn't yet speak,
your blunt pointer a question, an answer,
command, until five years in
Chloe lunged, teeth bared
at your small hand—
I lied on the release forms
for someone to take her on trust
as we had, from a breeder
who crossbred birds where
a peacock screamed on the lawn
and our soon-to-be dog bit
the edging that fenced her in—
so eager we failed to see her
spunk as runt anger the small
cannot live without, but you learned
so when the hamster died, your hand
blew out the backdoor glass and
now our cat is dying from old age
or a growth the X-ray can't detect,
science being less exact than fear
or wonder, his back knobbed as a rosary
—oh pet him, you who chose a hermit
as your patron saint; my prayer
a lonely abacus—my dog,
I can still hear her howl.

French Creek at Sunrise

Outside the cabin where I've come alone,
a squirrel cracks a branch, a small bird pipes

now, now, now. You're four,
at the ocean's edge. In your left hand

a fragment of shell smooth or ridged
as wings flung back like chicken feed

my grandmother scattered, seed potatoes
my grandfather returned to dirt.

What we need, we hand down. I filled you

with sounds; the first word you read aloud,
letter by letter: *Gulf* on a gas station sign.

Silence, the gulf I wanted you to cross.

When you asked, *What is how,*
I couldn't say. My head full of *What*

will become of you. What did I give but
drills and demands for high marks.

Last summer at Cape Cod, I watched
you, a grown man, teach a boy

to skip shells—a meditation you taught
yourself. Your future clouded

as a bowl of sea glass. A crow ratchets
like a man tightening a screw in the sky.

Tell me you are happy.

Teaching My Children to Drive

All children are potential
mistakes, by which I mean

accidents playing bumper cars
in utero or traffic, not looking

off into the distance, crowded
by the present; from the corner

of the eye seen too late, future's
glint off metal. Children, do not

be afraid. I am the state
trooper who writes my anger

in invisible ink. I know
the dividing line—dashes

that telegraph change
& speed. I will break

my promises, tell you
the world is safe, parenting

all burst & brake & traffic
jams. I am the horn, the hand

that leans on it; from ignite
to growl, from impact to scrap

heap, loss I cannot concede.
Signal when you turn. Use brights

on country roads. Charge
your phone. Watch your

mirrors. Don't drive on empty,
love. Buckle up. Merge.

Free-For-All

Bagged in the garage, my dress wedding-ready—
raw beige silk fine as papyrus, capped sleeves
pearl-trimmed, size nothing I'd wear again.

In the bag since '88, a gift teddy bear
in bridal gear, its headdress wedged in tight;
mine a false halo I ditched after my father skipped

the father-daughter dance; what we had not
practiced he didn't want to chance. Now old
as my father when he let me go, I offload

the blue garter, ruffled slip, shoes so small
they could fit a child. Let one make believe
a simple walk down an aisle ends in rainbows—

I won't be disillusion's bride. Forget the crying
flower girls, Aunt Betty's purse sunk in
the baptismal font she mistook for a glass tabletop;
that woman from the church rummage sale

who appeared beside us like Carol Burnett
with a mop; little Russell, his pudgy leg
stuck between interlocking pew chairs,
screaming through the *I Dos*. Shit happens—

it overflowed the aisles on the cruise
we didn't take; we took the recommended route
down the mountain pass and our brakes failed.

The overlook saved us. We're given what
we don't want and there's always a record:

my phone recording the inside of my purse,
and out the bus window, closeups of the Adriatic
ambushed by bush after bush after bush.

Two

Left Field

A mouse birthed her young on the engine
of our Pontiac Vibe, her pinkies safe
under the hood that seldom left the drive,
their panic then on the ride down I-95,
tiny snouts and paws wind-whipped
above firing pistons. Before your run,
you grope for your hat in a basket of gloves,
a short leap from *It was right here* to
Where has it gone? Hatless and cold,
you set out, headstrong as birdsong
chipping at snow. I wish I was that fearless.
Last night, in the space before sleep,
your head pressed the cartilage
guarding my heart. I held you, one
of three wishes; the others, our children
who outgrew our passion play and the chrism
a priest rubbed in to oil them for luck.
So many wishes go unmet. The mechanic said
he left them in a field behind the shop.

Doldrums

Sanctuary of Our Lady of Fátima

Behind the Basilica, an expanse almost empty in the rain. You and I take
shelter in the chapel; for two escudos, we light and place tapers along rows
of prayers wick-blackened, sputtering. In the plaza, a woman and man in
black; his umbrella above her slow-moving as a mast. She wears knee pads,
crawls on them, her rosary knotting her fingers, each knee an *o my Jesus,
forgive us our sins*. Who does her penance save. We are two facets without
a spine. Your neck warm on my hand. Huddled in your coat, I don't ask
what you pray. We walk on shadows here. Lúcia, Francisco and Jacinta
peer down at us from cathedral-high panels to where the Virgin came.
Does Mary listen better to pain?

Church of Slump & Weep

My body is a station with tracks. In this dark nave,
sour with urine and ruin, the aisle is a river of trash:

laces, spoons, needles, stubs, candle wax.
Mary, what mercy there is, let me feel

the warm light of your leaded silhouette:
my eyes shadowed rose, my torso a russet drapery,

blue a luster on my arms, my lips.
Did you know a man's mouth can foam

like the sea when he takes his last breath?

Fire Alarm

The diameter of a scream
is four inches

blasting through
blinking yellow, the same

diameter as the dead raising
their copper voices; at 5:30 a.m.,

his normal waking hour,
I rose frantic, and moving

through confusion the way
the fatherless can, I fanned

the alarm beating the air
as if my touch could soothe,

as if his face was the wall
I waved to.

On Franz Josef Glacier, December 31
Kā Roimata o Hine Hukatere

The helicopter blades our sudden uplift
along the valley wall. Under our crampons
that stake us where we list, water trickles
like blueing to bleach the underworld
we avoid; our breath white, the sun crests
serrated peaks and ice into stillness foreign
as moonscape, all of us in regulation gear
set apart by colored hats, scarves and mittens.
How at ease our guide seems, navigating unseen
paths, taking our pictures. Everywhere time
is blue until it isn't. The wind bores down,
picks up speed. The helicopter comes.
First to arrive, we're last to leave. Why
is vacation when we choose to take risks?
This Holocene glacier downwastes
under our feet. Everything ablates;
underneath its frozen tongue, water moves.
The guide tells us the mountain peaks
called arêtes mean fish bones in French.
I think of the Ötzi mummy, how it felt
for him to freeze. At least we wouldn't be
alone. The guide points across the slope
to a small orange tent, sides heaving.
This is not what we signed up for, to be
stranded or worse. Our helicopter
shudders beside the raw cliff face.
Nature answers only to itself.

Cycling by Brandywine Creek

Hidden crickets rasp their wings. Cicadas
keen the air. Bike wheels circle, gravel-crunch
a familiar score I mull in my sleep, teeth grinding

against the guard protecting them from
themselves. A squirrel stutters like a dolphin
lost in a tree & I lose myself to homespun

sounds: coins gallop free from pockets
in the clothes dryer; arguments we have
sneeze over & over, ferocious as allergies

that shiver the joists. The dishwasher,
when it ends, plays the first three notes
of *Camelot*. I ache where my dreams

kicked me last night. Why is joy so brief
a jingle between shows? Even a stone
unmoved in water knows how to chime.

At a Workshop on Grief

I palm a rock, its torso
creviced green between breasts,

shoulders veined and falling
into air. It feels heavy as myth,

as if Niobe on her cliff,
crying when snow melts,

has landed here. What can I learn
from her pride and its children,

her fourteen griefs? I have
enough of my own.

Elegy for a Family Photo Buried in My Desk

There I am, that long-ago girl,
a wilted flower Hank Williams might have loved
had he been in the front hall, yellow flypaper
and its winged black dots limp by the screen door
where family faces, all upturned, glisten

no more. Gone the cousins arranged by height like von Trapp
children on the stairs. Gone my aunt's square dance skirts
we wore as choir robes, waists around our necks,
our legs braced for the downbeat of Susan's hand

at the piano footing the stairs. We sang *Amazing
Grace, How Great Thou Art,* Russell's high tenor
not yet breaking, his mother's pride now gone
and gone all the indulgent laughter when we false start

three times, our faces urgent and red
with that moment's heat we hadn't learned
to dance around. All gone.

Gone to Jesus, the house where we sang,
an electric cross flanking its east side.

Saving Grace

How many times my mother marched
my mouthiness to the bedroom. Voices
and silverware muffled, I was banished

from the only country I knew: my family
seated around the table, hands like spokes
wheeling the lazy susan. Wonder Bread,

meat and potatoes, carrot coins dripping butter,
always gravy. That day in my habit of fast
turning, I spilled my chocolate milk again,

turned my father back into his father's rage,
made worse by dawdling in the hall. I heard him
barrel towards me and looked. Flip-flop in hand

caught on his big toe, he began to bunny hop.
Kitchen laughter, his sheepish look, delivered
him back to his hungers, his plateful.

Devil Bunny

His name was Napoleon. His habits that summer
gnawed me with rage, that randy white buck
my daughter left for safekeeping.

He would not honor books bordering the bed, leapt
them like a steeplechase; atop the mattress,
his whiskers a semaphore: *stop me if you can.*

At her place, my daughter had given him the floor
and free rein to chew a Coach bag, an orange shag rug,
one worn suede boot.

But faced with my limits, her pet adopted rabbitude.
Unswayed by dulcet tones or treats, he snarled and spit
till I tossed him by the scruff into his cage.
We battled for weeks.

On Facebook, our daughter in a swan dive
between cliff and sky-blue Aegean, became
a question mark. A week passed, then another
with no word. I pictured her
riding behind a stranger, a motorbike

vanishing into the Balkans. That summer
I needed to matter, but Napoleon wanted
to hide, his world upset as mine.

When I found him under the bed
peering from behind the barrier of garden fencing
meant to keep him out, I gave in.

Let him wander free on newsprint. Swept up
after him. Isn't that what Buddha would do,
give loss space and time; our détente,
one part surrender, two parts loneliness.

Margot

I gave you my past so you could have
your own. In utero, my blood
a dead end you pushed off

from. I cannot blame you
for leaving. Just as air travels
the body's sieve, we're not meant

to stay still; every breath a wave
goodbye. Yet my body retains the gnarl
of you in its aging, your lying-in

a biology the mind cannot claim
except in the past tense & even then
just a guess how the body found

straw & twigs & grass to make a nest,
the concept of a child like a bird
Paul Klee painted inside a head. Intimate

with purpose, we galloped together
into waking, into sleep. I wish now
I could visit the past as you did

the Lascaux cave; the rust bison
full-bellied on delicate legs,
deer horns veining the rock face

like rivulets, what those makers made
as homage to the coursing world,
I want to feel again—that swelling

awe you felt as ancient hands
stenciled on the cave wall waved
to you as you had waved at us

from your pod in the ultrasound.
Will winter ever end? Next year,
if I am here, come back.

Niobe Talks Herself through Winter

I hang where Mount Sipylus descends. Here
my mouth is prisoner, my arms raised in surrender
(how the heat of grief can make a body cold).

I am the one vengeance chose, the Valentine
stabbed by fourteen arrows. How do I stanch
the bleed? I hold tight my children as seeds

snagged in ice, emblems for what we know
too late of love and custody. Here I fall,
here I catch, here I wait.

Chicken God

Each morning I pivot
        the barnyard, calling chick-chick-chick

like a lawn sprinkler scattering seed.
        All foot and sound and feed, I am All

to the brood that clusters round, but to my
        crawling son who ploughs the oak floor,

head down like a horse furrowing the hall,
        I am alien. My feet slapping,

I race to catch him though
        he pushes off, not talking

not listening, the doctor says maybe
        delayed, common in boys. Nothing

to trust but worry, I am a god
        learning how hard it is to pray.

Window: After Diagnosis

While you sleep, nothing
out that dark poster stirs; I impose a
filigree of words that ring
and blazon what I believed and
now do not, their fading some
abundance lost. After drought, salt
stars the earth, hard as rice
the wedding couple leaves in
their wake, years cascading the
shift like the cull and call of surf's white
break—a sole worn thin shoes
a hole tonight, a cold music.
Something knows what I don't. I stalk a
coda, empty-eyed as a doll.

Manifest

71 migrants in a refrigerator truck, Austria, 8/2015

Sealed in this dark asylum
we rock in the wake
other rigs throw off.

At my daughter's birth
trees shook their rattles,
what joy—but here in
this clatter of throats,

she is lost. Around us,
lungs and guts collapse.
Her breaths coast to a stop.

What I have I hold.

After Driving Him to Work

My return is sluggish
in morning traffic.

Days are short
as memory. I forgot

to order his medicine.
When I am gone, who will

do better than me? I pass
an empty smokestack,

a billboard for cancer
spouting hope, birds like finials

on cold streetlamps.
Who will watch over him?

The light's green. I move on.

Three

In the Back Seat on I-70 When God Comes to Me at 12

Who's to say it isn't so, fog rising
off the Susquehanna at dawn, misting
the mountains; or maybe it's

mountain fog falling into the river
as sun notches the peaks of the Alleghenies

and climbs down through dense firs,
waking what nests in them and me—

earth's silent rotation, singing
even now across the span

of valleys, dim tunnels, past
sheer cliffs and rockfall, down

into the hard plains of Ohio
toward rain, corn husks shaking
dry their hair in afternoon light.

To Myself in the Modigliani Painting
Girl in Pink

The brush caresses my chin
        outlines my face
                my braids relax
almost weightless on my collarbones.

What my eyes take in, their apertures wide
and watchful as a cat's—

        goldfish swimming
                shadowless in its bowl

                a nylon stocking that has run
                        itself down shopping

        rabbit from a distance
                a furred rock on the green—

Are all my memories from that time
        sweet as crumbs of brioche

and closeted in that plain shift,
        does my heart still clap its schoolgirl hands
with erasers that dome the air with chalk?

Oh to capture life before the after.
        Before the butterfly, the cocoon.

Summer Stock

See the rickety house, the mosquito-fed lake.

Coffee perks up and filters the air.

Women sip their old resentments and talk low.

When the men return, they part the steam rising like stage fog
     from the grass.

If the screen door slaps like a man clapping another on the back,
     it means fish.

Children wake from sweat-sleep, tumble out.

See a striper, maybe a clutch of crappies, a smallmouth bass.

Next comes the wooden stand like an altar, the hose and bucket.

Watch the beheading, guts slit and spilled, the boat of bones
     parted from flesh.

On the cookstove, crisp-frying potatoes and onions.

The lovers trail in, what's between them clinging like static.

Letter to Her Husband in the Next Room

If all the world were you and me,
would we ever be enough? You engulf
the latitude and longitude of me
as a tree does its sun-making
shadow. Soft, the carpet that warms
my feet upon rising. My robe you
bought is a silk scene: peacock feathers
fan my back, and in front, I cinch a mist
of skylarks; as if fore to aft,
I wrap us together. Coffee you made
dark as a well fills me. Mouth
to cup, I think of us. The lightning-
struck red oak still blossoms.

The Love-Life of Animals by Wolfgang von Buddenbrook

Someone before me has lined in pencil the passages that interest them.

I interrupt your TV watching to tell you
    the hen pheasant generally so drab in her brown dress
    assumes male plumage thanks to sex hormones.

Lying on the sofa, your slender ankles crossed, arms behind
    your head, you have given yourself to the World Series,
    though neither is your team.

Your eyebrows don't lift their frown.

During a Viagra commercial, I read, *the castrated male*
    butterfly ... shows equally tempestuous desire.

"Who knew they still had urges," I say.

You shake your head. "Why don't they ever bunt?"

I tell you that bower birds construct a kind of dance floor
    to zigzag around until
    the male's pertinacity has its reward.

Knowing how often your non sequiturs spoil the big reveal
    on my shows, I add, "Who does that anymore?"

You wag a finger.

Vipers rub their pheromones on the ground to attract mates

who climb aboard. I imagine Shalimar at my wrists
wafting you to me.

The dog lifts her head expectantly.

In nature, choice is not always but is frequently possible.

The World Series may be seven games long.

Weight Watchers on Tuesday

I discover Africa in my fry pan, the unmistakable jut
of Morocco's west hip, its topography scrambled
in eggs and cheese, all sunrise and heat.
Today you leave for Buenos Aires,
exotic whereas I am a known function,
a hand turning a vintage egg beater.
Serving you, I relay how rain once left
an outline of South America on the driveway,
how the Singapore orchid survives
despite my negligence. I want you
to believe we still live in wonder;
romance, a mirage so close we can
climb the stairs to reach it.

No One Visits Dhërmi, Albania in April

We're the first guests since summer.
From our winter-cold room, we head back
into slashing wind and rain.

The manager has invited us in. She's put out
extra chairs. We crowd with her elderly parents
before a massive fieldstone fireplace.

She heats Turkish coffee on a small stand,
flame blue under a red enamel pot, metes
with careful ceremony its bitter richness.

The mother in black wears
on her face the hunger of another
winter almost past. Her keen eyes will

words from my daughter, this new language
jumbled in her mouth, her face alight
with risk. Soon to be parted from my girl,

I take sip by sip, a picture of this.

DNA Test to Identify Victim of 1944 Hartford Circus Fire

Lift from the bones I left all the risk
& hungers the Big Top could feed a girl:
the roustabout, his greasy thumb like a forbidden
   liniment on my ticket stub; the trickle of

sweat from white-faced clowns, their hoses
freshening sawdust; the dunged dirt of elephants.
Search me for dusky peanuts roasting
   my tongue; the man's sweet, sharp whiskey

tipped from a flask, talcum powder clapped from
high wire by the Flying Wallendas, our crowded
breaths we hold to behold them—
   the match that falls and catches.

Before the spotlight fills with smoke & after,
as flames begin to lick, search me for panic
as fire-fed paraffin drips from canvas, scalding
   screams, unskinning us:

the corncob pipe & its lipless man, the fallen
child, her clothes curling back like fading petals,
her eyes dark & uncomprehending as daisies,
   the tent pole snapped like a toothpick.

In me, what was or never:
the milky sweetness of a toothless baby,
the smell a man's head leaves on a pillow;
   all is tinder.

My vowels like penitence rise, though I don't know
what I'm guilty of. Search me for the traces
I leave, my body sky blue as wick to flame, a slurry
        like cotton candy, bubbling up & rendered.

Armor

What you can't keep, you can't protect,
I challenge you. Try to hold the floaters
in your eyes. They disappear like protozoa
we crawled from, or wayward

children—I covered mine in the human
version of contact paper for Halloween,

a brown hoodie strung with running
stitches I twisted hundreds of pipe
cleaners around; that tedious labor,
a porcupine. Even with face paint
no one guessed what she was,

a metaphor they hadn't learned
I wore in a Gilbert & Sullivan
operetta, where I romped as an extra
where no bears belonged.

My *pièce de résistance* I saved
for my son; with red shoelaces,
cinched a crab's bulging pinchers
to muscle his thin arms, to armor him.

What was given, shrugged off. Even
with candy, both kids sour in photographs.

Mall Run

I jockey for our place in line to see Santa,
though I know we don't belong. Straining like
Blitzen, my son spins on his harness and leash,
his face splotchy from sobbing.

Past Thanksgiving, it's packed.
All I Want for Christmas blasts above crowds
lugging packages, plowing the runway
with strollers like frantic passengers.

All I want is his picture with Santa, this child
who never cuddles or calls me anything.
I hiss, *We'll get french fries later, settle down,*
but he flails and bucks, revving
to high-pitched scream. Parents gift us
the evil eye and chandeliers point icicles of blame.

Where is the Santa for adults?
On his lap I would say, *Give my boy back
his speech, his look-at-me look, his sleep,
his play.* With your twinkly eyes and Ho ho ho,
jolly him back to who he almost was.
We stop traffic as I wrestle him
to the floor. Around us, a chorus of sneers.

I'd like to yell, *What are you looking at,*
when what I really want is to disappear—
me at the reins with my son, taking off
in a sleigh over Father Christmas, the open mouths
below on Concourse A. By Macy's, I'd scatter
coupons like snow, and zooming past Lego,

open the bomb bays and let the presents drop,
then climb into space, where all is silent—

the earth, safe as a distant ornament,
its light and dark, its swirl.

His fit has made other kids cry
but I don't care. *We're going*, I say.
I wrap my arms around my son,
more love than aggravation,
more tourniquet than hug.

Niobe's Fortune:

Land is always on the mind of a flying bird.

Fourteen times my children
        broke me. Fourteen times I pushed them
to slide between my legs as prophesy.

                One I named: *A dream you have will come true.*
                Another: *You will make your own happiness.*

Other names dim, my winter memory
        opaque as milk glass, a child's breath

                                    fogging a window

to make a heart. Ask not what I could have done
        to prevent the carnage, my boasts

        useless as ticker tape. What mother
would not choose to strive, to be
                proud of her young. What god

can judge who has not so labored. I left
        my children as carrion for vultures, their screams

tattooed in my throat—cliff-borne,
my grief a shroud no one names

                              swelled and broke—

bright leaves fall like hands,
the one who clung to me last:

Joys are often the shadows cast by sorrows.

To My Son Gone to War

I fight your four-cornered screen,

my call to dinner lost in the din
of bombs and downed men.

Did Super Mario down pipes lead us
to this *Call of Duty* where you die

and die again, when it's life
I want to keep you in?

What labor foretold, the push
of head against bone, and

following a suctioned plume, breath—
how your birth cry bloomed

to curdle time. I was your first
casualty. Your newborn hands,

tight-fisted as fiddlehead ferns,
hung heavy as bell clappers

as you grew. I cannot blame you
for playing soldier to kill or maim.

I know the thrill of waiting for what's hidden—
the boredom, the blast, the pain.

I am on the losing side,
but still yell, *I have mac and cheese.*

Saving What Struggles from Sidewalk to Grass

Slim but firm, it wriggles free,
an ampersand's *don't touch me.*

A snakelet, newly hatched, senses
in my clasp a beak—and absent a mother,

knows what to do. Humans, too, can live
with abandon. Doesn't every mother

choose the one she can ignore? My daughter
said, *You are why I didn't want to come back.*

Putting Your Children Back Where You Can See Them

Bullets skitter from cobblestones into sky,
from shells into turrets; planes loop their runs
in reverse. Bodies jerk and slump back

into being. One by one, your children rise

from where they fell, viscera snug
under skin, veins humming.

They walk unaware again.

Sky ushers back clouds and birds. Your staples:
bread and eggs, nectarines back in hand.

You are not less than. You are a mother with hunger to feed.

Onlookers, who hid like flies watching,
become people again. Espresso leaps
into demitasse, pastries half-eaten onto plates.

Words waft with aromas; apricots, sausage.

One by one, market stalls unsplinter and fill.
Customers inspect vegetables, intent on
the day's bargain. Your boy shouts his fury

at a soccer ball, your daughter runs
her hand over a bolt of magenta cloth.

No onlookers point. No planes
begin to howl their bestial descent. You finger
artichokes nubby as turtle skin, mandarins

dimpled with sun. You wave to your children.

Naptime

Forget daisies, their blown-black centers,
petals like children picked off

in a game of duck duck goose. Forget
broken families, stick hands never

to reach each other; let children file out
hand-in-hand like paper chains. Give back

the dog his nose, his bone, the pet turtle
chewing lettuce in class. Keep all

the shooting stars on tests, the arms
of superheroes kissing their chests. Mark

everyone present. Forget
the empty chairs, the closets where

children hold their breath, cupped
hands around hearts made of ears.

Great Green Room

Since we cannot meet in this world, let us agree
To meet in *Goodnight Moon*. I will hold
The red balloon as if it is a trigger
So you remember me. Here where nothing fades,
I will hold you in wonder like I did before.
Reading between the lines, I will explain
How long it would really take the cow to jump
Over the moon using Bernoulli's principle.
You will let me go on for several pages before
You interrupt, precious with laughter. Your turn,
You point to anything. I name it wrong
And pretend to be upset like I used to,
Though here there are no mistakes
You can't correct. No danger the mother bunny
Cannot protect against. The blue night closes
Us in with its curtain of moon and stars.
Are you tired, my love? Let us lie down
Where the bears have made rugs. Outside,
There may be men with guns, but
The fire is warm. And the finger that hovers
Like a drone does not seek us. In this room,
We are innocent. Listen: children call out
The names of things. Comb. Brush.
Bowl full of mush. They are so certain.
So safe in what they know. But we cannot stay.
The blue mantel clock has time only for sleep.
And we must not disturb the dreams
Of the young. I feel the book cover us
In sheets like a shroud. Though you beg,
We cannot meet in this world. Hush, child.

Four

Accidental Snapshot

We hold cherry water ice, Reno's
in blue script on the panel truck behind us;
cousins, uncles, me, my pigtailed daughter
by the Ford Dynasty, my toddler son
in his grandfather's arms lurching
toward the photographer. My husband
asks who the laughing woman is.

After You Call from the Airport

I open the closet to be near you,
the jacket you left.

I put my face on your shoulder,
take in your wooly salt & pepper musk.

My hands, like children, slide down your lapels.
I hold you close as you bumble over cornfields

leading to Chicago & know this
is love: how full an empty coat feels.

A House Chart & the Men in Them

I make a chart of him or him
(the qualities I like, ones I wouldn't choose),
each man a house & each trait a room

where I stand & ask myself if I could live
in a bungalow or split-level, which one,

& which man would give me space or hem
me in so close I'd wear him like Spanx;
would his Tabasco touch turn bland

or could he be my daily salt & pepper,
his blandishments a salve or an irritant

like cheap toilet paper; if I was blue,
who would text a thumbs up, who
let his body be my sofa cushions; whose bed

a game of hide & seek or chess where only
one wins; his funhouse laugh—

would it consign me to the basement
or his asides replay the Greatest Hits Of;
would he push all the buttons

on an elevator or choose a point & drive
in a nail for a picture. Would

every wrong be a prison or forgiven?

Animal Hospital

I'm lying on the floor with my dog.
We've never been in this room.
She lies on a cushioned mat curled into herself,
at rest with what is now.
I didn't know I would love the mat
that was worn into softness by the weight of those before.

I didn't know I'd love the baseboard view,
the linoleum that mimics wood, the stool
with its merry-go-round wheels, the flip-top bin,
what's no longer needed tossed in.

I didn't know I'd love the palm in the corner
losing its fronds. I pluck the yellow ones
and lay them in the dirt as if it is a pyre,
as if I have a right in this place
to put something else down that barely holds on.

I didn't know though I knew; I have this habit
of wanting to make certain the uncertainty
of the world, though everyone knows love is
a gamble like a stray dog in a cage. Ours slept
years with us, pushing the covers with paw and nose
as if our legs and trunks were a tree for her to nest.

How did I not know how much I love dogwoods
blossoming the wind out the window. The sun
glints off parked cars and those that pass.

Dogs bark in other rooms, but I don't mind
their vigor, their collars like love locks
on a bridge, committing them to another.

I never knew. The stillness of night broken
by sighs in a house, how a spare branch
in fall becomes calligraphy inside the moon,

and perverse my joy at paper lanterns left to drift
in a lake meant to lift spirits who stayed, who passed.

So many languages people speak for love.
What an irony that dogs understand
the most important one. My dog's eyes
say *face it*, this asphalt route, poorly marked,
that turns to gravel and darkness.

Beached

A sun-raked morning, sand cool, tide low.
Gulls boomerang past the window.

Come with me, I say. You ask why
I hunt for shells when we have basketsful

back home. You roll over in bed. Nothing stays
the same; not love promised, or weather.

I follow the wrack line, the blanket fringe
of brown pods and broken fans,

air sharp with salt-sweat. I was
an invitation once, our bodies wrapped

around each other like seaweed, my thighs,
my curves making smiles. *Explorer, kiss me*

here, I said, *and here*. We ran naked into
surf's shock, let salt wick our clothes dry.

I have left behind risk, become
the startled woman with her dog

we streaked past on the beach.
Do you recall that time we were rich

in shells—one day lightning whelks,
next day sand dollars, our children

nearby, your hand in mine. I didn't think
I was chosen for loss, but who isn't—

our parents gone, a daughter overseas,
a son gaming away loneliness.

And what of you I left grumbling in bed,
your back curved, face slack on the pillow.

I pass a stranded jellyfish, pick shells
I cannot name. When we watch *Jeopardy*,

I say *Of course*, after the right question.
Who's going to take care of me, Dad asked

as Mother drifted into wordlessness. Am I already
less wife, more burden? More and more,

you fill in the blanks for me. At high tide where
I walk, waves swell, keels sway, fish flit and vanish.

On the Yangtze

Nets stand like fences
      awash in the river

Ancestor fish
      —finned palominos—
nose mollusks, rope-bound

Currents sway
      in the sun's pink wash

On my fingers, nicotine—
      on my shirt, ash
           where it slept

I watch one water
      become another

Every Day Something Different

Yesterday I heard the noise wind makes
       in a storm—not falling
leaves, or their rattle—there was

no wind, only a moving insistence like
traffic muffled in snow; not snow, a blizzard

of wings, a parabola of starlings
       risen from trees to churn the cold, and

today an eclipse, the moon sanded by earth, one thin
       bright handle unattached; we are

detached from so much, but when
       a Knock Out rose survives the frost
like a megastar blowing the crowd

       a kiss, despite monsoons and fires
and unnatural disasters, every day
       something different shakes loose

what we know: the older I get,
the simpler I become: *wow* I whisper
       as awe ghosts the porch.

Psalm for the Unasked-For

To give you the *yes* of the world I have not
          felt: sun spackling my kitchen pothos

with its blanching warmth, the moon
          fuzzing willows scored by wind.

 I have not stood my ground
          in ocean; swept under, have fought

to reach you, salt dried on my skin
          like a crystal palace the palm reader

promised me. Children now beyond
          preach: swallow the oyster sweet with

brine, blueberries dotting whipped cream;
          bloomerang my *no* with snow-bound lilacs

spring uncorks, listen: birds accordion.

If James Wright Came Back

Let poems fly willing as sonar
to the cave of you.

Let them nest in pockets you didn't
know how to fill. Forget

for a while, your friend face down
in the tide, spine to the sun like

a toppled crucifix. Stand cliffside
and feel the stars sift silken as flour.

Relax your clouded look. Let dreams
milkweed in, their nectar a haven for

bounty and bees. Forget the hooded one,
needle-slumped, who became

a corner tragedy. And what of the girl
on Water Street, her fierceness, her thin

frame a hanger for rent? Where night
is a backyard tent, make a flashlight

of poems. Sing her the O of wood, sky
piped with birds, prairie grass

a windy susurration—gone a moment,
the traffic's jerk and cough, the ravenous

sway of barter and john. Let no wounds
or war, bottle or threats, palsy

the hours. Walk into the world you left.
Let your words make diamonds of rivets.

Consider Silk

an oil-rich bath, a second skin
giving trouble the slip; in your hands
the full-length glide of a mink coat—
or would you choose a silt-rich pond,
forget in bucolic's calm the brain-
wasting amoeba that lurks; picture
a marble floor after rain, a ladybug
webbed weightless before the shift
to shroud and venom, Isadora Duncan
throttled, her scarf taut in a hubcap—
turn instead to a mirrored wall you can waltz
clean across, flax you can field for miles,
or closer still, an orchid's pouting lip:
Give me my child, his newborn skin,
air's first touch he parachutes in,
his heart streaming a road that empties
and fills, learns to forgive my rough hands.

Linda Shows Me James Galvin's "Two Sketches of Horses"

Her fingers drag and splay to hold them still. Days before, her horse had died.
Gruesome, she said,

his femur broke jagged through muscle and blood, what comfort her hands
on him now gone;

his body chained and hoisted up, legs dangling like roots or wood chimes.
From her window,

drag marks, white hair she will collect for birds; under one of her nails, dirt—
she has turned

the page to yearlings, a girl in wildflowers; before her, ghost horses running
like geoglyphs, one lifting off.

Another Way to Land

I've been falling lately, roots
        and throw rugs knocking me

down, the ground hard and familiar
        to my feet, now familiar

to my face. Once I trusted gravity
        to hold me upright, running

into marriage, the hard measure
        children take of who you are.

Last week, I held out my arm to
        a Harris hawk, wings wide as

grace landing to feed. Before
        falling, earth was a place

to step on. Now it has bled into me
        branch and feather, flower

where death will carry me.

November

I walk past field stubble, stalks
black and broken, corncobs chewed

down to rust; in the swamp, dead
eucalyptus where cormorants hunch.

This wetland, so cold and forbidding
cradles what lives: frog hearts

slow in their silted sleeping, mud
turtles prone on a bog of leaves.

My body ages into mystery. I face
dread, a snake skin in the grass. Molting

has shed its muscled menace, head-
to-tail a fogged diamond pattern,

delicate as church light.
An empty leash, I drag it home.

Canticle for Remnant Days

1.

The sun, ragged & red, salsas the sea:
the mollusks, the octopuses, all its creatures
puppets of salinity. Don't we have license
to forget the handwringing of hours

that fill & fall as salt in its cellar?
Where Lot's wife was reduced to brine,
nothing grew. Leave the pickaxe, its deep-set mines,

likewise, the cubicle and badge.
Let evening rollercoaster like hair
free of its net. Remember night is the rock
where you beat your clothes clean.

2.

The remnant day walks with you.
        Guard its aches & banes as you would

a boxer's hands. Tenderly wash
        the knuckled bruises, the scrapes closing

to scab. In the last gape of sun, bind them
        white with sheets. In the gap

where curtains part, the moon, blank
        as agape, whispers.

3.

I am the *and* between sun &
none, the needle that closes
      the chain-link gash.

Do not heed the blood. It will stop itself
as moon does the sun, heedless
      of its falling. In the tilt to night, all

is prayer: moonflowers open their parasols
& tomorrow carries us to bed, counting down from ten
      our waking breaths.

Notes

"Of the Safe House, Now Empty," is inspired by Susan MacMurdy's mixed-media collage, *Dream House, Later*.

"Window: After Diagnosis" is a golden shovel. The last word in each line comes from the first line of "What Was Promised Me," by Cecilia Woloch from her chapbook, *Earth*.

Franz Josef Glacier was named for Franz Josef II in 1865. It replaced the original Māori name, Kā Roimata o Hine Hukatere, which means "Tears of the Avalanche Maiden."

"Great Green Room" is written after Dennis Nurkse's poem, "Every Great Novel Ends in Sleep."

"Animal Hospital" is written after "Things I Didn't Know I Loved" by Nâzım Hikmet.

Acknowledgments

Grateful acknowledgment is made to the editors and staff of the following publications in which these poems first appeared, some slightly changed or with different titles.

Apple Valley Review: "Summer Stock"
Bear Review: "Burrs"
cahoodaloodaling: "Family Quartet"
Colorado Review: "Great Green Room"
Delmarva Literary Review: "Chicken God"
Gargoyle: "*The Love-Life of Animals* by Wolfgang von Buddenbrook," "A House Chart & the Men in Them," "Linda Shows Me James Galvin's 'Two Sketches of Horses,'" "Another Way to Land," "Rule of Jaw"
Kestrel: "Animal Hospital," "To Myself in the Modigliani Painting"
Mom Egg Review: "Niobe Talks Herself through Winter"
Naugatuck River Review: "DNA Test to Identify Victim of 1944 Hartford Circus Fire"
One Art: "In the Back Seat on I-70 When God Comes to Me at 12," "November"
Rat's Ass Review: "Afterward"
Red Wheelbarrow: "Mall Run," "To My Son Gone to War"
RHINO: "After an Argument with a Friend"
Riddled with Arrows: "Margot"
River Heron Review: "Devil Bunny"
River, River: "Cycling by Brandywine Creek"
RockPaperPoem: "Every Day Something Different," "Of the Safe House, Now Empty"
Split Rock Review: "Canticle for Remnant Days"
Summerset Review: "Manifest," "The Body's Certainty"
The American Journal of Poetry: "Church of Slump & Weep"
The Broadkill Review: "After You Call from the Airport," "If James Wright Came Back"
The Crafty Poet II: A Portable Workshop: "Elegy for a Family Photo Buried in My Desk"
Two Hawks Quarterly: "Heading West on I-80," "Putting Your Children Back Where You Can See Them"
UCity Review: "Beached," "French Creek at Sunrise," "Naptime," "Night Swim"

Walking the Sunken Boards: "Letter to Her Husband in the Next Room," "On the Yangtze"
Watershed Review: "Fire Alarm"

"DNA Test to Identity Victim of 1944 Hartford Circus Fire" won first prize in the 11th annual *Naugatuck River Review* Narrative Poetry Contest.

"Mall Run" was a finalist in the 2017 *Red Wheelbarrow* Poetry Contest.

"*The Love-Life of Animals* by Wolfgang von Buddenbrook" was a finalist in the 2019 *Art of Stewardship* Poetry Contest, Chestertown, Maryland.

"Great Green Room" won first prize for a single poem in the 2020 National Federation of Press Women Contest (NFPW). *Walking the Sunken Boards* received second prize from NFPW for a book of poetry.

I am grateful to Patric Pepper and Mary Ann Larkin at Pond Road Press for their care in publishing this book. Thanks to Tara Skurtu for her guidance in the development of this manuscript. Thanks also to Tara, Diana Goetsch, Michael S. Glaser and James Arthur for their kind words about this book. I am grateful for encouragement from Mark Leidner, Cecilia Woloch, Richard Peabody, Bruce Weigl, Gerry LaFemina, Diana Goetsch and Sherry Chappelle. Thanks to the Delaware Division of the Arts for its generous support, to JoAnn Balingit, Delaware's poet laureate (2008-2015) for her early guidance, and a shout-out to writing pals Wendy Schermer, Maria Keane, Maria Masington, Sharada Manns, Jane Strobach, Billie Travalini; to Devon Miller-Duggan and the crew at Friday Night Writes and thanks to Jamie J. Brunson, Shannon Connor Winward, Pat Goodman, and Betsy Cullen for their astute feedback. A special thanks to my coauthors and retreat trio: Wendy Elizabeth Ingersoll, Gail Comorat, especially Linda Blaskey, whose mentorship, quick wit and derring-do have enriched my life tremendously. Above all, gratitude to my parents, who let me paper my bedroom walls with poems; love to my children, who allow me to ransack their lives for material, and to my husband Mark, who encourages and ignores me, in equal measure, so I can write.

About the Cover Art

I first saw Judy Kirpich's work in a special exhibit at *The Delaware Contemporary* in Wilmington, Delaware, and fell in love with *Conflict No. 1*. Judy graciously granted me permission to use her work as cover art (see www.judykirpich.com). The excerpt below from her artist statement speaks to my own process as a writer.

"I love the juxtaposition of spontaneity and precision. To get a composition to look free flowing and gestural demands great control and exactness. This is my holy grail and I still have not cracked this nut. But I continue to try."

About the Author

Jane C. Miller's poetry has appeared in *Colorado Review, RHINO, Apple Valley Review, UCity Review, Kestrel,* and *Bellevue Literary Review,* among others. A winner of the *Naugatuck River Review* Narrative Poetry Contest and two fellowships from the Delaware Division of the Arts, three of Miller's poems were selected by the *Poetry in Transit* program for display on buses in Luzerne County, Pa. She is coauthor of the poetry collection, *Walking the Sunken Boards* (Pond Road Press, 2019) and coeditor of the online poetry journal, *Quartet,* (www.quartetjournal.com). She lives in Wilmington, Delaware with her husband, son and dog.

Also from Pond Road Press

Messages, by Piotr Gwiazda
Parts & Labor, by Gregory Hischak
Radio in the Basement, by Bernard Jankowski
Familiar at First, Then Strange, by Meredith Holmes
Shubad's Crown, by Meredith Holmes (out of print)
Blue Morning Light, by David Salner
Human Animal, by Anne Becker
Crooked Speech, by Sid Gold
Tough Heaven: Poems of Pittsburgh, by Jack Gilbert (out of print)
Walking the Sunken Boards, by Linda Blaskey,
    Gail Braune Comorat, Wendy Elizabeth Ingersoll
    and Jane C. Miller
Season of Harvest, by Linda Blaskey & jim bourey
Guest of Time: A Memoir in Poems, by Greg McBride

Colophon

The typeface used for the front cover, spine and associated text on the back cover is P22 Wedge from the P22 Type Foundry. As a wedge font, this typeface features triangular serifs at the end of strokes for a change-up look and pleasant readability.

The interior text and cover comments are set in Adobe Garamond Premier, designed by Robert Slimbach and released in 2005. Slimbach has won many awards for his typeface designs. Among those awards is the prestigious Type Design Award, given in 2006 by the Type Directors Club for Garamond Premier.

This book was printed in the United States of America by Lightning Source LLC, a business unit of the Ingram Content Group.

www.ingramcontent.com/pod-product-compliance
Lightning Source LLC
Chambersburg PA
CBHW020210090426
42734CB00008B/1001